A NOTE TO PARENTS

When your children are ready to "step into reading," giving them the right books—and lots of them—is as crucial as giving them the right food to eat. **Step into Reading Books** present exciting stories and information reinforced with lively, colorful illustrations that make learning to read fun, satisfying, and worthwhile. They are priced so that acquiring an entire library of them is affordable. And they are beginning readers with an important difference—they're written on four levels.

Step 1 Books, with their very large type and extremely simple vocabulary, have been created for the very youngest readers. **Step 2 Books** are both longer and slightly more difficult. **Step 3 Books,** written to mid-second-grade reading levels, are for the child who has acquired even greater reading skills. **Step 4 Books** offer exciting nonfiction for the increasingly proficient reader.

Children develop at different ages. **Step into Reading Books,** with their four levels of reading, are designed to help children become good—and interested—readers *faster.* The grade levels assigned to the four steps—preschool through grade 1 for Step 1, grades 1 through 3 for Step 2, grades 2 and 3 for Step 3, and grades 2 through 4 for Step 4—are intended only as guides. Some children move through all four steps very rapidly; others climb the steps over a period of several years. These books will help your child "step into reading" in style!

Text copyright © 1991 by Stephen Krensky. Illustrations copyright © 1991 by Norman Green.
All rights reserved under International and Pan-American Copyright Conventions. Published in the
United States by Random House, Inc., New York, and simultaneously in Canada by Random House
of Canada Limited, Toronto.

Library of Congress Cataloging-in-Publication Data
Krensky, Stephen. Christopher Columbus / by Stephen Krensky ; illustrated by Norman Green.
p.   cm.–(Step into reading. A Step 2 book)   Summary: A simple account of Christopher
Columbus's first voyage to America.   ISBN: 0-679-80369-6 (pbk.); 0-679-90369-0 (lib. bdg.)
1. Columbus, Christopher–Juvenile literature.   2. America–Discovery and exploration–Spanish–
Juvenile literature.   [1. Columbus, Christopher.   2. Explorers.   3. America–Discovery and
exploration–Spanish.]   I. Green, Norman, 1934–   ill.   II. Title.   III. Series: Step into reading.
Step 2 book.   E118.K74   1991   970.01′5′092–dc20   [B]   [92] 89-62507

Manufactured in the United States of America 10 9 8 7 6 5

STEP INTO READING is a trademark of Random House, Inc.

Step into Reading

Christopher Columbus

by Stephen Krensky
Illustrated by Norman Green

A Step 2 Book

Random House 🏠 New York

It is August 3, 1492.

A new day begins

in a busy Spanish harbor.

Three ships—

the *Niña*,

the *Pinta*,

and the *Santa María*—

are starting out to sea.

Someday these ships will be famous.

People will know their names

five hundred years later.

But the men on board

cannot even imagine that.

They are afraid of getting lost.

The ocean is a great mystery.

How big is it?

How long will it take to cross it?

What is on the other side?

Will they ever get back to Spain?

Christopher Columbus is not afraid
of getting lost.
He is the captain of the *Santa María*
and the leader of the voyage.
Columbus knows a lot about the sea.
He is a navigator and a mapmaker.
Now he dreams of becoming
an explorer, too.

The rulers of Spain—

Queen Isabella and King Ferdinand—

believe in Columbus.

They are paying for his trip.

Columbus promises to find a new route from Spain to the Far East.

India, China, Japan—the Indies!
Lands of gold and valuable spices!
If he succeeds, Spain will be rich.

Columbus knows the world is round.

Why not travel to the Far East

by sailing west?

But the world is bigger

than Columbus thinks.

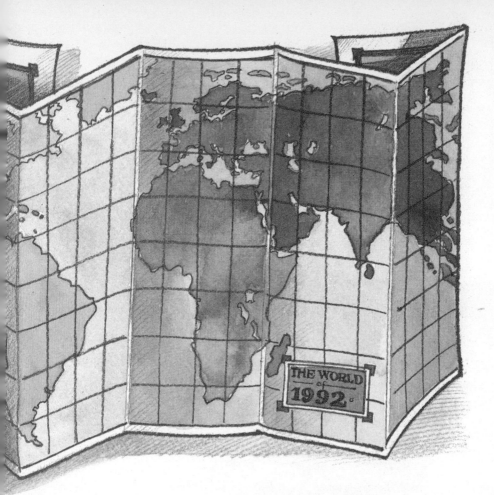

And there is something else

Columbus doesn't know.

Two huge continents

lie in his way.

Nobody in Europe

knows they are there.

Soon the sailors cannot see land.

Now they are *really* afraid.

What if the wind stops blowing?

The ships have no motors.

What if there is a storm?

The ships are small

and made only of wood.

What if they run out of food?

They cannot go back for more.

What if they are in danger?

They cannot radio for help.

But the weather is good.

The wind blows steadily.

The sea is calm.

The ships are loaded

with food and water.

There are extra sails
and spare wood.

In fact, so much is stored below,
the sailors must sleep on deck.

There are ninety men in all—

about thirty on each ship.

Most are sailors,

but there is also a doctor,

a carpenter, a goldsmith, and

an interpreter who speaks Arabic.

There are even some boys

to help the sailors.

Weeks and weeks go by.

Now everyone is tired *and* scared.

Tired of eating salt meat.

Tired of seeing nothing but ocean.

Tired of being stuck

on a tiny ship.

One night a ball of fire

blazes across the sky.

The sailors watch it fall

into the sea.

Is it a warning sign?

Should they turn back?

Are they going to die?

But Columbus knows

it is just a meteor.

"Sail on!" he tells them.

And they go on.

One morning the sailors
see another strange sight.
A blanket of seaweed
covers the ocean.
Will the ships get stuck?
The sailors are afraid.
But not Columbus.
"Sail on!" he cries.
And on they go.

They have been at sea

for almost two whole months.

Where is the land Columbus promised?

Columbus points to the birds

flying overhead.

He points to the leafy branches

floating in the water.

Land must be nearby!

More days go by.

The sailors complain loudly.

Who cares about finding

a new route to the Indies?

They just want to stay alive.

Columbus must turn back now!

If he does not,

they will throw him overboard!

Columbus begs them to wait.

Just three more days, he says.

The first night goes by.
On the second night,
the lookout on the *Pinta*
sees something ahead.
The moonlight is reflecting
off a sandy beach.
"Land! Land!" he shouts.
The message is sent
from ship to ship.
It is October 12, 1492.

As the sun rises,

everyone can see an island.

This must be the Far East!

Three boats go ashore.

The sailors are so happy

to be on land,

they kiss the sand.

There are people on the island.
Columbus calls them Indians
because he thinks he has reached
the Indies.
He names the island San Salvador.
He says it now belongs to Spain.
But the island really belongs
to the people who live there.

The Indians have never seen
men with swords.
Why have they come?
What will they do?

Columbus gives the Indians

shiny beads and tiny bells.

The Indians give Columbus

soft, cool cloth and colorful birds.

People in Europe do not have

cotton or parrots.

The Indians are wearing gold rings.

Columbus asks questions with his hands.

Where does the gold come from?

The Indians do not understand.

Columbus sails further west

to look for gold.

He visits other islands.

He meets more Indians.

Most are helpful and friendly.

They live in grass houses.

They sleep in rope beds called hammocks.

They travel in long boats called canoes.

Columbus sees many new things.

But where is the gold?

Early one morning

a strong wind

drives the *Santa María* aground.

The ship is wrecked!

Columbus moves to the *Niña*.

But there is not enough room

for everyone on the tiny ship.

Many sailors must stay behind on the island.

Soon the *Niña* and the *Pinta*
are ready to sail back to Spain.
The ships are already loaded
with many new kinds of food—
corn, potatoes, peanuts,
papayas, avocados.
Columbus has also forced
six Indians to come with him.
People in Spain have never
seen Indians.

On the way home

the weather changes.

Day after day

fierce winds batter the ships.

Huge waves wash over the decks.

Even Columbus is afraid

of sinking.

On March 15, 1493,
Columbus finally reaches Spain.
The voyage has lasted
thirty-two weeks!

Columbus rides on a mule
to visit the king and queen.
Everywhere along the way
people gather to cheer him
and to see what
he has brought back.

Columbus is a hero.

King Ferdinand and Queen Isabella

listen to his stories.

They call him

"Admiral of the Ocean Sea."

They believe he has found

a new route to the Indies.

They have no idea that San Salvador

and the other islands he visited

are not part of the Indies at all!

For the rest of his life,

Columbus never knows

how truly great

his discovery is.

He has really found a new world—

a world that no one in Europe knew about.

It is called America!